I DARE YOU

FRAZER BROOKES

DEDICATION

To my mother and father, you are my heroes, I love you.

CONTENTS

ACKNOWLEDGMENTS

Travelling around the world, spending countless hours away from loved ones to help the businesses of others is not so easy. At times it is exhausting and draining. I wouldn't be able to do it without my fiancée, Svetlana. Thank you, I love you.

I'm eternally grateful to my parents, Julie and Simon, for saying yes to this industry many years ago and sticking with it through the tough times. I don't know where I would be today without you both.

To my extremely tall Italian friend Vincenzo Sannipoli, thanks for making what we do fun and for collaborating with me on hundreds of webinars, events and live calls. I appreciate you, brother.

Being a coach inside the Network Marketing space can be a very lonely place, especially when there are only a few other people who share the same values as you. Rob Sperry is one of those people. Thanks for all that you do, mate.

Huge thanks and love to Eric Worre for his help, feedback, and honesty with this book, and being one of the most consistent people I have ever met. I believe we live in a time where generic training is needed more than ever, and I think it is no coincidence that the name Eric is in the word "generic". Thank you.

Finally, this book is for everyone who has believed in me on my journey so far and continues to support my mission to raise the professionalism of network marketing done online and to unite the industry to make it sexy again.

CHAPTER 1

I DARE YOU

I was born in 1988, and my Network Marketing career began in 1987...

How the heck does that happen?

Well it's 1987, my mother and father, Julie and Simon are at their home in Southport, North West of the UK, in a house that they owned. Times were tough, they had no money. In fact, my dad often said to me, "Frazer, we were so broke, we couldn't afford to pay attention!" So in order to pay the bills they decided to live in one of the rooms on the ground floor and rent the five bedrooms upstairs to complete strangers.

Anyway, one morning, my dad goes into the kitchen to find an open newspaper left on the kitchen table. Usually he wouldn't even notice, but this time was different. He spotted an image of an Aston Martin sports car, with three words above it!

"MLM MLM MLM, I drive an Aston Martin, you can too, call me on XXXXX"

What could MLM be, my dad wondered...

Make Love Monthly?
Make Love Mondays?
Make Lots of Memories?
Make Lots of Money?

The curiosity had gotten the better of him so he decided to give the number a call. But, it went to voicemail, so instead of leaving a message, he saw there was another smaller advert next to the one of the Aston Martin, so he called that number instead. He was greeted by a man named Neil, who after explaining that MLM really stood for Multi Level Marketing, invited him to attend an event in Blackpool.

The day of the event arrived, and my parents were sat in the packed out venue where over 500 wildly passionate adults were sitting full on energy and excitement. I was also in the room that day, in the womb. They then began to watch people just like them walk across the stage to collect huge bonus checks and one of the most powerful thought processes in Network Marketing happened to them.

If they can do it, so can I.

And that was that, they decided to become independent distributors on 26th October 1987 and I have been with them every single step of the way.

Growing up around both parents building a Network Marketing business has been the most incredible lesson for me. The sacrifice, freedom, drama, victory, people, travel and development just to name a few things.

It wasn't easy though, unfortunately the first company they joined was not their last. They were distributors of that company for less than three years, before moving on to their second home, and nine months later it was time to move again!

But the third time something had to change...

They went to work, learned the skills, but applied them more than anyone else. Were they pro's? No. But they soon became some of the best Networkers in the world.

I saw my parents earn over $10,000,000 in Network Marketing as I was growing up. I travelled around the world with them to visit their team of over 156,000 distributors and I had been listening to cassette tapes of Jim Rohn, Les Brown and Zig Ziglar everywhere we went.

However, there was a problem.

I knew Network Marketing was a legitimate and serious opportunity to earn an extra income. I knew it wasn't a scam or a pyramid scheme. I had seen the freedom, fame and fortunes that could be made, as well as the people my parents were associated with. But, I also saw what my Dad had done to be successful.

Normally if you could access the exact steps a millionaire had taken to have success you would get excited. In today's world people charge thousands of dollars for this sort of access. But, I knew my Dad, he is crazy, a huge extrovert. I was not!

I didn't get that "If they can do it, so can I" feeling.

Why?

Because I had watched him go through three things every single day when he was building his business:

1. Rejection
2. Failure
3. Speaking in front of others

Those were my three fears. The fear of rejection, the fear of failure, and the fear of public speaking...

I continued to watch my parents help hundreds of people reach their goals, some big, some small. I soon realized that what someone sees as a small goal, others see as a big goal. So, in fact, every goal is a big goal.

It was now my 18th birthday, and I was about to receive my first ever official "pitch". I knew how the compensation plan worked, I had taken the products since before I could remember, and I knew the system to success. Plus, I would have a mentor who has reached the top, but will also have an extra special reason to want me to win, and win big!

But, I said no.

My Dad accepted that. It was the first time I had ever seen my Dad take no as the final answer, it was as if he knew I was going to say no, and that I wasn't cut out to be a Network Marketing professional.

My parents still to this day will tell you that they thought I would never do Network Marketing because I was the shyest person they had ever known.

However, every three months my Dad would bring up the opportunity, there was never any pressure and I always appreciated him for that. He let me get on with things.

Four years went by. I went to college, then onto University to study Construction Management, learning how to build buildings, instead of building businesses. All the while knowing that I would only ever be able to earn a fraction of what my parents earn. But, I was an introvert. Surely I couldn't do what I had seen my Dad do, acting like a crazy person in front of a crowded room, getting people tell him to get a real job, seeing him be let down by others, and have friends turn jealous and sometimes bitter.

Then it all changed...

It was Thursday 8th April 2010, and I was sat at my computer studying for my final ever University exam, I had 6 days to go, and I found myself wonder over onto Facebook™. I had received a message from a complete stranger which I completely disregarded, but it triggered something which I had learned from my Dad.

"Frazer, are there more people on the planet that you do know? Or that you do NOT know?"

I thought if I could contact complete strangers, without having to be that crazy person drawing circles at the front of the room then perhaps I could win!

I looked into my mirror and pointed to myself while saying "Go on Frazer, I dare you".

Looking back at that moment I must have be possessed, if anyone had seen me do that they would have called for the doctor.

Anyway...

I walked from my room into my Dads office and the following conversation occurred:

"Dad, I am ready, I want to join!"

"Why now Fraz? What's changed?"

"I am going to build it all online using Facebook ™"

"Frazer, remember, success leaves clues, there are no companies or distributors who have had success using online methods, everyone is just spamming!"

And he was right, back then there were no companies, coaches, mentors, webinars, seminars, books or events showing people how to build a Network Marketing business using the internet or social media.

I went back into my room, looked at the mirror, pointed to myself and said "Go on Frazer, I dare you!"

Something was pushing me to do it, my Dad finally allowed me to join, and that was that. I officially became an independent distributor in the Network Marketing industry!!!

Within about seven minutes of joining I had created the master plan, it was genius, how had no one else thought of this. I had found a way where I could contact more people in one day than my Dad could in one month!

So here it is, the master plan...

I wrote down the following message:

"Hey Bob, I noticed that you are also part of (enter business page or group here) and as we are like minded I think it would be awesome to connect with you. In fact, I have an amazing opportunity I know you will be interested in. Here is a link to the presentation (enter YouTube™ link), let me know if you have any questions, but if you want to get started now, go to this link (enter my signup link). I am excited to work with you soon! (Enter thumbs up emoji)"

I would then copy the message, find someone on a business page or group, then paste that message. The only thing I had to remember was to change the name from Bob to whatever their name was, then hit send. There were times when I called women Bob, whoops.

It's a numbers game, that's all I kept hearing at the events I was going to. So I knew I had cracked it.

A few weeks had passed, and nothing had come from it. Yes, I had a few people reply with some questions, but mainly people were blocking me, reporting me, or sending me abusive messages back. I even spent some time in Facebook™ Jail.

The master plan didn't work, it was over, how was I going to tell my Dad that I was going to quit. I couldn't just avoid him like I had seen others do over the years. I decided the best thing to do was to face him head on.

I walked into my Dads office, it was the exact same walk I took when I was full of excitement and energy when I wanted to join, but this time I said, "Dad, I am going to quit, it's not for me, no one wants to join, I have sent a message out to hundreds of people, and had nothing".

And his response was the four most powerful words I have ever heard and is one of the reasons why I am in the position I am today, writing this book.

"Let's rob a bank!" he said.

Part of me thought he had really lost the plot, the other part was excited, I didn't have any other hopes so why not.

He continued, "what do we need to rob a bank?"

"Well, we would need a balaclava, get-away car, crew of people and probably a shotgun".

He leant forward in his chair and replied, "Frazer, we aren't actually going to rob a bank, but if we were, what would we seriously need?"

I simply said, "we would need to know where the vault is".

"Yes, you need to find the vault" my dad said.

He then went on to explain that "people are like banks, they are well secured and they need careful planning for you to break into them. You need to get the blueprint, but you also need to know what is in the vault. You definitely don't want to rob an empty bank."

What he shared with me in that talk helped me to create a true master plan, one that was exciting to do, easy to follow, but that seriously worked.

Using what I learned that day I was able to create a business of over 300,000 customers, all using social media. But more than that, I was able to travel the world, meet the woman of my dreams, and become someone who I would never have believed I could ever be.

You are going to be learning the exact strategy I used and many others around the world have used, so that you can share this with anyone you know in Network Marketing so they can truly have the success they deserve using online methods.

As I mentioned earlier, I am on a mission to raise the professionalism of Network Marketing done online and to unite the industry. I love everything about Network Marketing it has changed my life, and now it is time for it to change yours too.

So I dare you, pay attention to what I share in this book and you too can radically improve the way you build your business using social media.

CHAPTER 2
I DARE YOU TO GIVE IT A GO

I first studied Attraction Marketing when I was about ten years old. My dad was advertising in the national newspaper for people who wanted to make an extra income working from home.

He used an advert to attract people to call him, then he would sit in his office taking their calls.

During the school holidays, from time to time, my dad would shout out "we've got another one!"

Me and my brother would then go with my dad into the dining room to find a table with eight stacks of paper on them. Each stack was made up of hundreds of pieces of paper containing information about a certain part of the business. We then had to take one piece of paper from stack one, then the same again from stack two, and so on, until we had eight pieces of paper. We then put the pile we had accumulated into a shiny black folder and then place it all together into an envelope.

My dad would then write the address of the person on the envelope then at the end of each day drive to the local post office to send all of the packages off to those wanting more information.

He was attracting people using advertising, sending the information out to them, then following up to see what they liked best.

This was attraction marketing back in the 90s...

There is a big difference between prospecting and marketing, and at the end of the day, we are involved in the Network Marketing industry. We have to learn how to market our product or services, and also ourselves.

Prospecting is reaching out to your friends and family expecting them to join.

Marketing is attracting your target market to take a look at what you have.

Prospecting could be tied to selling. Marketing is likened to sharing.

Prospecting is being the hunter. Marketing is being the hunted.

However, you need to do the prospecting when starting out. You write your list, you learn how to contact them, then you encourage them to check out a video, come to a presentation, jump on a call, or speak to your business partner, then you follow up.

But I want you to understand this.

The long term money isn't necessarily in your original list, but it's in the skills you develop from your list.

Yes, there are people who have crushed it using their original list, but the masses struggle. Every top income earner that I know of has gone through their list, whether they have succeeded from it directly or not is another question.

But the panic that sets in is incredible when you ask someone to make a list of people who you know, love and trust, people like your family and friends.

Have you ever heard someone say to you "yeah but I don't want to sell to my friends and family!"

Why do they say that? Simple, because we are taught that your business is built by prospecting people on your list.

There is also a huge percentage of people who have written their list but not contacted many of the people on it. Why? Because they believe they shouldn't sell to their friends and family.

Network Marketing is not selling. It's sharing. Kind of.

For example, whenever I had someone in my organisation say to me "oh Frazer I'm going to smash this, I've been the number one in sales in the company I work for", almost instantly I'm turned off. For me that's the Network Marketing kiss of death.

They try and treat Network Marketing like a selling business.

The reason companies choose the Network Marketing industry is so their advertising budget is directly tied to revenue that is created. No revenue, no advertising spend. They rely on the reps to share what they feel to be the power of the products, people and purpose, they don't sell the products on shelves in stores.

Now, you have to go through your list, no doubt about that, simply to get the skills needed to succeed.

Skills like facing rejection, objection handling and hearing it's a pyramid scheme to name a few.

"Oh go and get a real job"

"Uncle Bob did that, it doesn't work"

"Only the people at the top make all the money"

If you learn to not let your loved ones distract you from creating a better life, then when you speak to new contacts it won't bother you what outcome you face.

But remember, your business will truly begin when your list ends.

If you master the art of marketing then you'll never run out of people to talk to, and having that ability will give you the opportunity to build a long lasting, consistent business.

Trying to convince people you know and love to join your business or buy your product will most likely end in tears, so don't force the process. If you feel that you are having to force it then I want you to think of this saying:

Prospecting is like farting, if you have to force it, it's probably crap!

You are looking for people who are looking. You are sharing a message with people and seeing if they would also want to share.

When prospecting your target market is your list. Your friends, family, colleagues, school friends etc.

When marketing your target market is someone you can relate to, maybe another mum, sports fan, travel enthusiast, couple, animal lover etc.

They say "you can't choose your family, but you can choose your friends" well, in this business "you can't choose your initial list, but you can choose your target market".

I want you to think of the following story from this point onwards on how you can use attraction marketing to build your business.

You're driving down the motorway, along with many other cars, and all of a sudden you see a big new cinema, and decide to go inside. There are two types of movies. Good ones, and bad ones.

The bad ones, you walk out of half way through, then there's the ones that are so good, if you are needing the toilet, you try your best to hold it in because you don't want to miss anything.

Now, because you are loving the movie you are sat in your seat, but you get hungry, "if only I had some popcorn to go with this movie!"

In walks in a man who works for the cinema, he is carrying boxes of popcorn and he walks up and down the aisle, not saying anything. You reach out to him and end up buying a box of popcorn.

Now let's look at the same story in terms of Network Marketing.

The motorway with the cars is traffic, the cinema is your story, if it's bad people won't be interested, if it's good, people will stick around and be engaged. When they enjoy what they are hearing they will want to buy the popcorn which in this example is your product or service.

So your goal, is to create traffic, to a compelling story, and have that offer ready for when the time is right.

I have used many platforms, but the one that consistently gets me the most traffic, and best engagement with the story I'm creating is Facebook™.

Although what I will be sharing throughout this book works for all platforms, I will be using the most popular social media platform for my examples.

I dare you to give attraction marketing a go. Be warned though, using social media to build your business is a part of the process and not the entire process.

CHAPTER 3
I DARE YOU TO CREATE THE RIGHT MINDFLOW

What the heck is mindflow?

Well, although having the right mindset is important, the word "set" to me has always sounded like concrete. So why not call it mindflow. "Flow" like a river, forever adapting to its surroundings, a force of nature.

I remember when I was about sixteen walking passed the lounge and there was a meeting going on. The flipchart was out, I saw circles with peoples' name inside them and people on the edge of their seat. I was intrigued as my Dad was getting to the stage where he would get super passionate.

"This business works 100% of the time for 100% of people who give it the time. You just have to decide whether you will take it seriously or not."

When he said that, one woman raised her hand and asked, "Simon, how long will it take me before I can make enough money to treat this as my job?"

I was interested in the answer, I always loved seeing my Dad handle peoples' questions.

"This is not a job; this is a business that can earn you job replacement income with time."

The woman actually said it wasn't for her, she was looking for a job.

I learned a lot by listening into that meeting that day. Understanding that Network Marketing is not a job, it is a business.

You should not track your hours and expect to receive similar income to your day job. Instead you track the completion of small daily tasks, which over time, will compound into significance, impact and fulfilment. For most that will be income, for others it will be transformation, and for the minority it will be the satisfaction of seeing other people win.

I asked my Dad more about the struggles of getting people to think differently, and he simply said to me something that has stayed with me ever since.

"Frazer, in the beginning you do a lot for a little, and in the end you do a little for a lot!"

The reason why I tell you this is because when you get into building your business you might be asked by your partner "how much money have you made?" and it will be likely that it will be little to none.

So instead of saying "not much", simply say, "it's a business, most take a few years to breakeven, I am already super close to that, so I am ahead of the curve".

When you begin to market yourself, using social media be prepared for it to take time, develop your skills, trust the process and never quit before pay day.

One of the things that I disliked the most in Network Marketing was the mindflow of giving something a year. "Ok Frazer, I will join, and see how it goes after one year". I would actually prefer them not to join. Do you get married to someone and think, you know what, I will give this a year and if my partner is up to scratch I will continue the marriage for another year. No, you are committed for the long term. The only real variable in Network Marketing is YOU.

Those who call it a scam have scammed themselves by not putting in the time and energy to learn the skills and take the necessary action.

If your company pays the reps on time, delivers the products in a timely manner, the owners are committed to build a legacy company, and there are people achieving what you would one day like to achieve, then the company you are with is a good one to get to work with.

You need to focus on the following formula:

Activity x Skills = Results.

If you put in all the activity in the world and neglect skill development, long term your results will be little. If you only focus on skill development and don't put it into activity, then your results will be slim, to none.

In fact, in school, we are taught that any number multiplied by zero, equals zero. The same applies here, zero skills, will give zero results, zero activity, will also give zero results.

I have something called the 1:1 rule. From this point onwards I dare you to ensure you don't stray too far away from the following:

Let's imagine we have to walk towards our goals, its directly in front of us, in a straight line, about ten meters away. Every time we spend one hour on personal development we will move our left leg forward. When we spend one hour on activity we will move our right leg forward.

Here's the problem…

The majority of us are stuck in a spin as we are doing hours and hours of personal development without taking action. On the other side, too much action without the skill development can cause issues too.

Too many people focus on their results over the course of a year. Your results are made up from the combination of your activity level and skillset, focus on them and your results will come.

Commit to the journey, trust the process, detach yourself from the outcome, and give yourself "as long as it takes" instead of "giving it a year".

Having been around Network Marketing my entire life, and social media the day it began, I have studied the statistics and even ran my own polls, surveys and questionnaires. Asking top leaders, newbies, CEOs, founders and other corporate members in the Network Marketing world. I found that the average person quits after just six weeks, however, the average person gets their first win, whether that be big or small, after eight weeks. To me that tells me that the average person who joins Network Marketing quits before pay day.

Social media is similar. If you start after reading this book, be sure to give it as long as it takes for you to get the results, it won't be an instant fix, remember there are no secrets to success, however there are systems to success. In this book you will learn the system that I was able to use and share that helped me grow my organization as well as the organizations of many leaders all around the world.

In Network Marketing the friendships that can be created are incredible. Like-minded people on similar missions can create bonds like no other. That might sound a bit crazy, but those of you who have a Network Marketing friend will understand.

I am fortunate enough to have a very close group of friends, I have known them my entire adult life, and even some from birth. But I also have friends in the Network Marketing world who I have known for less than three years and I am connected with them on an even deeper level.

When you are building your business using social media you have the ability to create friendships unlike any other. You will have the chance to not only meet people from all over the world, but create a network of friends who will help you when needed.

My philosophy when building my Network Marketing business was to:

Turn Strangers into Friends, Friends into Family.

There are more people on this planet that we don't know, than we do know. As Network Marketers it is your job to go and connect with the world, and that is the reason why the likes of Facebook™ was created.

Use it and you have the chance to build an empire you could only dream of. Abuse it and you'll be nicknamed a spammer, scammer or schemer.

I dare you to create the right mindflow by paying attention to this chapter, be unstoppable, adapt when you need to, and be open to learning new skills and putting them into action.

CHAPTER 4
I DARE YOU TO TURN LIKES INTO LEADS

In the world we live in more and more people are becoming obsessed with what others are thinking about them. So when it comes to social media, we judge our popularity on the number of likes we get on a post.

It even gets to a stage that if you post, and get no engagement in the first ten minutes, some might even delete the post!

In order for you to make money from your social media accounts there are a few things you need to know, I like to call them the four abilities to becoming free with social media.

Ability #1 – Increasing your visibility
Ability #2 – Raising your power of likeability
Ability #3 – Developing your influence-ability
Ability #4 – Growing your profitability

Let's go through each ability so that you can begin to take the steps needed to turn likes into leads.

ABILITY #1 – INCREASING YOUR VISIBILITY

In the social media world visibility is extremely important. In fact, if people can't find you, they can't buy from you. The more visible you are the more chance you have of getting new customers and distributors, which I will go into in the following abilities.

But, at the same time, "you should not confuse visibility with credibility", Harvey Mackay once said.

Now the social media platforms have complex algorithms which take into consideration thousands of actions to decide what content appears inside of the main news feed.

Although the algorithms are complex equations, what you have to do is actually very simple, most just over complicate it. So understanding how this works can lead to an increase in your visibility, so that's the aim of the game with this ability.

I like to break it down to a made up word called "FEP".

F is for Friends List. E is for Engagement. P is for Posts.

Too many people are simply adding the world, thinking that it's a numbers game, and if you have more friends on your list then you will have more success. But that is not true.

The number you need to work on is actually a percentage.

Your goal should be to genuinely connect with close to 100% of your friends list as possible, the higher that percentage the better.

Imagine if you went to a pub and one hundred people were there, you have never spoken to any of those people. You walk in, and no one really notices or acknowledges you, and you reach the bar with no issues. It's a lonely place.

Now, imagine that same pub, full with one hundred people, but this time, all of the people were people who you had connected with. You walk in, and everyone turns round, they notice their friend, some will stop you to have a chat, some will give you a hug, and hey, you might even get your drink bought for. It's not a lonely place, it's a thriving environment.

Social media platforms want to see this, a place where you want to go and you will never want to leave.

So your first step will be to remove those friends you have who you have no intention of connecting with, they don't engage with your posts, or perhaps they don't even use the platform.

Inside our community we share different ways on how you can easily remove the inactive people as well as the least engaged friends. I cover more on that at the end of this book.

Get that friends list optimized. Remove the dead weight then connect with the remaining people on the list.

Now onto engagement.

There are three things you can do extremely easy and right away that will help you with your visibility, and they are:

1. Reacting
2. Commenting
3. Messaging

When it comes to **reacting** this is simply loving on other peoples' posts using those emoji's. **Commenting** is straight forward too, if you like a post, why not comment on it too, people cannot like a like, so be more visible by commenting something relative to the post. Lastly **messaging** people is the most powerful. It is called social media for a reason, it is a platform for you to be social on. Almost all social activities require conversations, well using the messenger is the best way to converse.

If you are active, engaging and participating on your favourite social media platforms you will be rewarded.

Lastly let's take a look at your posts.

Your posts have a big impact on the visibility. But don't fall into the over posting trap. There is a saying "if people can't see you, they can't buy from you", and that is true, but if you post too often you will be competing against yourself in the newsfeed.

Think of it this way. A friend of yours goes to work at 8am, and doesn't get home until about 7pm. Meanwhile, you have been posting all throughout the day, let's say eight times. Now your friend decides to sit down in front of the TV and at the same time she goes onto her phone to do some social media scrolling.

Is she going to see all of your eight posts? No!

She might be lucky to see one.

I advise you follow the three hour rule, so stop over posting. Basically you should not post within three hours of your most recent post. For example, if you post at 9am, don't post again until 12pm, if you post at 4pm, don't post again until 7pm, and so on.

I will show you what to post a bit later on. But if you follow the above your visibility on social media will increase.

ABILITY #2 – RAISING YOUR POWER OF LIKEABILITY

Getting your posts seen is one thing, having someone actually engage with them is another.

I recently did a poll in my private training community asking if people notice the number of likes, comments and shares a piece of content gets before they engage with it. The response was staggering. Almost everyone said that seeing a post with a large amount of engagement makes them want to read the post, and engage themselves.

It's like going to a buzzing restaurant. If no one else is in there, and you are eating alone, it's not very fun. But if there are many people, lively music and great conversation, you don't want to leave.

Now this takes time, you can't make one post today and expect one hundred people to like it right away. Also, likes won't build your business, but following what I share later in this book will.

So in order to raise your likeability you have to focus on these three things:

1. Be Consistent
2. Create Conversation
3. Give Value

Like anything in life, if you consistently do it, results will show. In fact, Bruce Lee once said, "Consistency trumps Intensity every time". I prefer this saying:

"You can't have a shower on Monday and expect to be clean for the rest of the week."

So you need to show up daily on social media. If you post once a month you won't get far, so aim to post at least one piece of content a day.

As well as that, you need to create conversation inside of each piece of content. So if someone leaves a comment on one of your selfies, be sure to reply to it asking a question. For example, you post a photo of you and your partner on a Friday night, and your friend Mary comments saying "Have an awesome night guys!" You would then reply, "Thanks Mary, are you up to much tonight?"

What this does is it takes that post from one comment, to potentially many, therefore increasing the likeability.

The final thing is to give value with the aim of helping others. Network Marketing is the best industry in the world for helping others and if you use social media correctly you can help more people than ever before.

Zig Ziglar said it best when he said, "You have to give, to get".

Value can be something as simple as a quote, story with meaning, or even a live video. I will cover that more in future chapters.

So if you consistently create conversations around valuable posts you will notice your likeability will increase. It will take some time to build this up, but it will be worth it.

ABILITY #3 – DEVELOPING YOUR INFLUENCE-ABILITY

When you have increased your visibility, and your likeability is rising, you then need to develop your influence.

Influence is a word that has become extremely popular since social media became accepted worldwide. More and more people now are looking to become an "influencer". They create a big following, then monetize it.

The definition of influence is the ability to have an effect on the character, development, or behavior of someone or something.

The great thing about influence is that I can help you create it in six to eighteen months, whereas leadership can take many years to develop, and some are just not cut out to be a leader.

Another incredible thing is that chances are, you already have your vehicle to monetize the influence you will be creating.

Think of someone you admire and respect. In this example I will use Tony Robbins. If he was to call me and say "Hey Frazer, its Tony, Tony Robbins!" Everything would stop. He has that much influence over me that I don't care what I am doing, this call is my number one priority.

If he was then to offer me an opportunity, I would say yes before he has even asked me.

But let's go back a few steps.

Why do we look up to different people? Well there are a number of reasons, they are:

1. We want to live our life the way the influencer is living theirs
2. We respect their knowledge on a certain topic
3. We admire the success they have had in the same field we are involved in

I will share with you how this can be done in the next chapter, but the key test is if people come to you and ask you a question then you have the influence over that person.

It is usually created in one of three ways on social media:

1. You contact someone twelve times for at least twenty minutes at a time
2. Someone watches seven hours of your videos
3. Someone engages with thirty two pieces of your content

Contacting the same person twelve times is not going to be easy, and it will take a lot of time. You might not have any videos right now, or you simply might hate having to do them. So creating engaging content appears to be the easiest.

One of the best ways to grow a social media following, and build influence, is through documenting your life. Whether you are travelling, attending events, spending time with your family, just document it and share with the world. Lifestyle is good, value is great, being authentic is best!

ABILITY #4 – GROWING YOUR PROFITABILITY

So you know how to get your posts seen. You know how to get the engagement. You know the basics of how to create influence. Now it's time to discover how to monetize all of the above to grow your profitability.

I remember when I was starting out in Network Marketing trying to master the online ways, and I kept thinking, "it's a numbers game". So I just wanted to find people with huge email lists, buy them, then mail out my opportunity and wait for the sales to come in.

That never worked.

I didn't have the influence with that list, but also there was just no personal touch with it.

I get emails or social media notifications from Tony Robbins and Eric Worre almost daily, and I enjoy consuming the content, but if they were to message or call me it would be a totally different story.

So in order to truly grow your profitability with the influence you've created you need to get good at reaching out to people at the right time, and there is no better time than now.

There are 3 types of people to reach out to in this case:

1. People who like/love your content
2. People who comment on your content
3. People who share your content

The first type are going to be the least warm, they might just like it whilst they are scrolling. But you will notice with time that some people might be liking almost every piece of content you create.

You could say something like, "Hey Bob, thanks for loving my last post, how's things with you?"

Oh, and always end with a question, no matter what you say.

Next up are the people who leave a comment. Whether it's a bunch of emojis, or something more meaningful, perhaps they are giving their opinion. If its negative or abuse, delete it, you don't need people seeing that.

The people who comment are warmer than the "likers", they have taken the time to write to you, so be sure to reply to their comment and then message them privately to say something like this.

"Hey Bob, thanks for commenting on my last post, I appreciate that, how's things with you?"

Super simple, but effective.

The last type of people, are those who share your content, these are the most warm, in fact, they will be boiling hot.

Something you have said has connected with them, and they want others to see or hear it too. Keep a very close eye on shares that your posts get. You will want to send a message like this, "Hey Bob, thanks for sharing my last post, that means a lot. Everything good with you?"

By now you have probably noticed a theme. It's all about getting into the messenger of those who are engaging with your content. A big turning point for me was when I realised this:

Conversations come before Commissions!

With an increase in your visibility, a rise in your likeability and the development of your influence, when you message someone, maybe they have become your "fan", you can dictate how the conversation goes.

Just don't let it get to your head, always remain humble, I dare you.

It's now time for you to learn what you need to set up before you begin the daily method of operation that will allow you to not only create influence and have more conversations, but be able to duplicate throughout your organization so they know exactly what to do to build their business using social media.

CHAPTER 5
I DARE YOU TO HAVE A FACELIFT

So the first thing that needs to be done, is you have to make sure everything is all set up. I've always understood that a business is determined by the foundation that you set.

If you build a house on sand it will fall over. If you build it on concrete, solid concrete, it will last the tests of time.

So that's what we have to do, create that solid foundation.

I like to call it the social media facelift. The social media operation for you to look as attractive as possible online. And this works whether it's on Facebook™, Instagram™, YouTube™, and any social media platform.

Because first impressions mean a lot, and style beats substance these days, when it comes to social media, people will make up their mind if they like you and want to get to know you based on how you look online. It's a shame really.

I want you to think of it this way. You decide to go out one night, but to a random village nearby. You arrive to the village, and head to the dedicated food street. On this street there are

5 Italian restaurants, they all serve the same food, are the same size, and are all open. However, none of them have menus outside, and once you go inside you can't leave until you have eaten. Which one do you choose?

The one that looks the best or is the most busy, right?

Today, we tend to trust things based on its popularity, or how it comes across. Its appearance.

So this step in the process is fundamental.

In the online marketing world, there are websites known as "landing pages". Marketers drive traffic to a landing page, with the hope that you will give your name and your email address in return for something of value. Whether it's an e-book, an audio file, a video series, whatever it might be.

Now on social media, your landing page is your profile. So the goal is to get people to come over to your profile, like what they see, and then eventually follow you, add you as a friend, or engage in any of the content that you have created.

Conversions from profile visitors to new fans, followers or friends is the aim of the game. So what I encourage you to do, both yourself and your team should actually go through the social media facelift.

There are four key points for you to go through:

1. Have a clear profile photo
2. Have a personality based cover photo
3. Have a curiosity creating bio section
4. Remove any spam or unclear posts

HAVE A CLEAR PROFILE PHOTO

A good profile picture is simply a photo just of you. No distracting background, no distracting foreground, no partners, no pets, no children. And also, you should be smiling and don't wear sunglasses.

People need to see the whites of your eyes, and your teeth.

It should also be rather close up.

Now I don't want you to judge your profile photo by what it looks like when you're on your profile itself, but when you're commenting in different people's posts, what does the smaller version of the thumbnail look like? If it stands out, then fantastic.

If not, then if you have light hair and features, have a dark background, if you have dark hair and features, have a light background. Contrasting can help the small thumbnail stand out. Wearing bright and vivid clothing will help too.

When you get the right photo, stick with it, you shouldn't change it regularly. Get people to notice that one image, eventually they will fall in love with it and begin to notice you everywhere they look online.

And the final point to note, is you should actually have the same profile photo on every social media platform you're a part of. Don't confuse people with different photos that look different.

HAVE A PERSONALITY BASED COVER PHOTO

Your cover photo is the second image that you get to choose on your profile, now it's super important again because this is your social media billboard. This is where you can advertise anything you want. The problem is the majority of people advertise what they've got to sell as opposed to who they are. Think of it this way:

"You want to stop pushing pitches and instead pull people towards your passion".

How you do that in your cover photo is to use a website called Canva.com or Fiverr.com. Go ahead and create a sexy looking, professional, modern, clean cover photo that shows off who you are as a person and what you're interested or passionate about.

Mention your name and maybe two or three things about you. For example mine is, "Frazer Brookes, Network Marketing Ninja, Social Media Coach, World Traveller."

When someone then comes over to my profile, they know exactly what I am about and if I can help them, instead of thinking, "Oh wow, he's going to try and sell me something".

Curiosity will attract people to add/follow you. Advertising will repel people, and cause them to leave your profile.

HAVE A CURIOSITY CREATING BIO SECTION

Now the bio section. Whether this is on Facebook™ or Instagram™, this is actually the most important part of every profile when it comes to building your audience. Why? Because people are going to look at you on first impressions and go, "Okay, they seem legit. They seem cool." And then they're going to actually go and try and find out what it is you do. They will then determine what it is that you do by looking at your 'about me' section.

If you've got your company name blasted all over it, the number of friend requests and followers you get can potentially drop.

I know you should be proud of your company, but you can show how proud you are of your companies in different ways. I will explain how a little bit later.

I remember a time when I was about twenty five years old, my niece, Daisy, was one year old and my sister, brought Daisy round to the house to ask my Mum to look after her. Unfortunately, my Mum was not around at the time so my Dad had to take this challenge on of looking after Daisy.

All of a sudden my Dad comes into my office and said, "Frazer, you're going have to look after Daisy because I'm going out to see some of my friends."

My first reaction was, "Okay, that's absolutely fine. No worries." Then after the initial thought had passed I realized, "What am I going to do looking after a one year old kid? I've never looked after a kid in my entire life. Let alone a one year old."

So I put her on the floor, she was playing around with a few of her toys and I'm on the computer working away, speaking to people all over the world. The next minute I smell this awful, horrific smell. So I thought I'd open the windows and let it pass.

A couple of minutes went by, and Daisy had begun to cry. I remember thinking to myself, "What am I going to do?"

So I picked her up and I tried to calm her down. I shook her like I was making a cocktail. I had no idea what I was doing. I decided to smell her nappy and it was bad. It was really, really bad.

So I ended up putting Daisy on the floor and I actually grabbed my laptop, put it next to me, and opened the lid. I then Googled, "How to change a nappy?"

I had no idea what I was doing. The first step was to find the bag with the nappies in. Fortunately, I knew where that was because I had never seen my sister without this magical bag of glory, the bag that held the items to everything. So I opened the bag and found the nappies.

Step two, remove the nappy and dispose of it, and step three, wipe away any excess.

At this moment I am gagging, it's revolting.

Step four, clean the area. Step five place new nappy.

In that moment, when I needed the answer to something, I didn't want to look bad. I didn't want to be embarrassed by having to call my parents or my sister, and then have them panic, thinking, "oh, he has no idea what he's doing."

Instead I asked Dr Google. Because Dr Google knows the answer to everything.

And that's what the majority of people will do. When people come over to your profile and find out what it is that you do, when they don't know what a company is, or what it is that you do, they will Google it. So if you say, "Star Ambassador, Black Diamond Affiliate, Elite Level Five, with Company X", people will type in, "What is Company X?" And if you give the game away, you will lose.

One of the first things my father ever told me about building a Network Marketing business is:

"You want to tell people everything, but nothing".

On social media you want to tell people everything about who you are, but not everything about what you do.

For example, a Nurofen, if you have a headache you will take one because you know everything that it does. You know that it will help ease your headache. But you don't know the ingredients.

So instead of sharing your rank and company name. Say that you are a CEO, Director, Founder or Owner of your own business, maybe your team name or a business page you might have. Those titles are desirable and high in status, and so adds an element of credibility.

Also add where you live and where you are from, it gives another point that others can relate to. Whether they have visited there, have family there, or plan to visit. Maybe they just like the sports team based in that city.

REMOVE ANY SPAM OR UNCLEAR POSTS

Chances are, you are reading thinking one of two things:

1. "Yes, I have done the above"
2. "I have some work to do"

So the last thing for you to do before going into the social media daily method of operation (DMO), is to remove any spam or unclear messages you might have posted.

Perhaps you have photos of you drinking with your friends, remove them. Maybe you just have shared a ton of funny cat videos. You might have been tagged in a spammy photo promoting fake sunglasses.

You just need to go down about fifty posts, and work your way up removing any of them so when people come over to your profile the posts they see are going to match up with the message you want others to see.

Once it's done, it's done. Once you have that foundation, it's time for you to build your social media skyscraper.

I dare you to give yourself a facelift, it makes a massive difference and imagine a day in which people want to become Network Marketers because they are the ones who are the best at social media!

CHAPTER 6
I DARE YOU TO CREATE CONTENT (STEP 1)

Social media is all about telling a story through the content that you create.

The first step when understanding what content to produce is understanding your target market. Now a lot of people get confused with this, and they ask me daily, "Frazer, what is my target market?"

Well it's very simple.

Your target market is the person you are. Whether you're a Mum, Dad, family person, sports lover, you like travel, food, fashion. Whatever it might be, whatever you like, that's your target market.

There's the saying, "Your vibe attracts your tribe." Now you don't want to attract a tribe full of people about cats, when your love and passion is for dogs. Likewise, you don't want to be attracting a tribe full of women, if you're a man. Or if you're a woman, you don't want to attract a tribe full of men.

It will get very draining long term if you try and be someone you are not just for a financial gain.

You want to attract people who are like you, your people, the people who know your language, the people who know when you're being honest and truthful, that you're talking about the right things.

For example, my target market is Network Marketers who want to build their business using social media. Your target market might be other Mums or other parents who want to earn a secondary income. Or it could be looking for Mums, single parents, Dads, who want to travel less for more.

It could be Mums who want a secondary income. It could be Mums who want better skin. It could be Dads who want to lose a few extra pounds.

Your target market can be as crazy as you want.

In fact, a friend of mine had an idea for a group he wanted to launch.

So he asked me, "Frazer, I have a great idea for a group."

I said, "Okay. Well what's your passions?"

He began to tell me that he had a passion for women, and he had a passion for lamps, as in desk lamps. At first I thought, "Yeah, this is a bit strange."

But he said to me, "Well you say that the passion and the target market can be anything."

I agreed, it really can. He said, "I've got this idea for a group called Lamp Lovers. This is going to be a group, and all it is, is photos of women with lamps."

As crazy as it sounds, there literally is a market for everything. In seventeen months the group grew for zero to over 760,000 members.

Your vibe attracts your tribe, so we have to focus on only speaking about one or two areas of your life. Let's look at it like this...

You are sitting at home, and you're wanting to put a film on and watch it with your partner, maybe you've got a glass of wine or a cup of tea, whatever it might be. You turn to each other and say, "Ooh, what kind of movie do you fancy watching? Should we watch an action? Romance? Comedy? Thriller?"

You don't say, "Oh, I really, really want to watch the new adventure, sci-fi, horror, documentary, biography, action movie tonight."

No. It's one or two things because you know exactly what you're going to be getting from that movie.

The same applies with social media. You only ever really want to talk about one or two areas. For example, I only talk about network marketing and social media. Yes, some of the posts you might see from me might just be around the area of positivity, but it's helping the network marketing and social media community.

If you're a Mum, maybe you are going to talk about social media and business. Maybe you're going to talk about cooking and being a Mum. Maybe you're going to talk about travel and fashion. You will build an influence based around the content you put out on to social media.

I challenge you to get a piece of paper and a pen, and write down everything that you believe is your target market. Write down all the things that you would love to talk about, or you're currently talking about on social media. Whittle it down to be super, super specific.

A friend of mine, Rob Sperry, once said to me, "Frazer, niches to riches."

You only need a few hundred people to adore what you talk about for you to build a hugely successful business.

When creating content, you have to:

Constantly Create Curiosity, and not Regularly Raise Resistance.

Too many people are being salesy, they're talking about what their product is and how you can buy it, instead of saying what the product does, and the next steps to learn more.

When you sell you raise resistance, you push people away. If I was to go over to your profile, and all I saw was sales based messages, pictures of your product or "join my team". Would I want to go and add you as a friend and follow you? Probably not.

Whereas if I saw some posts that were highly valuable and created curiosity, maybe I wanted to add you, message you, follow you, to potentially see what it is that you do. That's the aim of the game.

There are six different types of content. You've got text, image, photos, stories, pre-recorded videos, and Live videos. Let's go through each one.

Text only, you'll notice on my profile, I use a lot of these. I actually use a lot of just text because it gets a lot more visibility.

The second type are images. These may be graphics, infographic, maybe quotes with text in them. They're great. They work really well on business pages and groups.

Photos could be selfies, photos of you and your family, maybe photos of where you are, maybe where your office is today. Social media platforms loves to show your family and friends what you're up to. Selfies with your partner out on date night work well on Friday and Saturday evenings.

Stories are incredible. They give you the chance to show your followers behind the scenes access into your life, it's like the back stage pass. Everyone wants to get the special access to their favourite celebrities.

Pre-recorded video, is fantastic because video is king. Video is the number one source of content consumed on social media today.

Live video gets the most engagement, it gets the most reach, it gets the most traction and awareness of who you are. Live TV shows tend to be really popular due to their engagement ratings. The percentage of a live show viewing time, is much higher than that of a pre-recorded show.

When you have established the source of content, you need to understand and follow what I like to call the RVL formula.

The R stands for Results.
The V stands for Value.
The L stands for Lifestyle.

Whenever you're posting from this point onwards, ask yourself, "Does what I'm posting give results of what I'm doing, value to my audience, my tribe, or does it show off my lifestyle?"

When I say show off, I don't mean, "Oh, I drive a red Ferrari," or "I have Gucci handbag," or "I make lots of money." I mean, the lifestyle that I'm living, is it going to be relatable to someone else, or is it going to make someone go, "Ooh, I'd like to have that in my life?" Without faking it 'til you make it.

Okay, so results. One of my favourite things to do on social media is to get to know people and their story. I encourage you to attend events, speak to people who are in your company, whether they're in your downline, crossline, upline. Get a photo with that person and get to know their story. Have a library full of peoples' stories in the same company, and use the same products as you.

What you're going do is every two weeks, you are going to make a post and say something along the lines of, "Hey, meet my friend Bob. Bob also uses the same products that I do, and I recently got the chance to meet him and hear his story. Bob was able to travel more for less. Bob was able to lose three kilos. Bob was able to reduce the wrinkles in his face. Bob was able to improve his finances. Be like Bob. Message me if you want more." Something like that.

It's important to show you helping other people get results, instead of your own results, because a lot of people out there will think, "Oh, it's okay for Mary. She's a superstar." Or, "It's okay for Samantha, she's been on that diet for nine months now." Instead, you need to show how you can help other people, because people will then start to think, "Ah, if Mary's helped three other people, or five other people, or 10 other people, maybe she can help me too."

When it comes to value you'll notice that social media, especially Facebook™, is becoming a heavily valuable resource for people. People are now looking for value more and more. They're looking for peoples' tips, instead of Google's tips.

I encourage you to get a little black book or even just the notes app in your phone. Start to note down any quote you hear. Whether it's at an event, you read it in a book, you listen to it in a video or an audible. Write it down. Put your own spin on it and produce, whether it's a text only based post, a Live video, recorded video, maybe it's an image with a quote in it, or even a Story. Giving value will improve your credibility, because people will begin to look up to you and start to think, "Wow, I could probably learn a thing or two from this person."

Lastly, is lifestyle. This is the easiest one because all you have to do is live your life. You don't have to have an exotic lifestyle to have an appealing lifestyle. What I mean by that is, there could be someone out there who wants a dog, and you happen to have a dog. You showing photos of you walking a dog makes them think, "Ah, I really want to have a dog one day."

I always think of it this way. Let's say I'm at the traffic lights, and I'm in the middle lane, and I am in a Volkswagen Polo. To the left of me pulls up a guy in a red Ferrari. All I'm thinking is, "Wow. That would be amazing to have one like that someday, but I probably won't because I make $30,000 a year, and one of those cars costs like $250,000. There's no way my wife would let me buy one of them."

Then on the right hand side pulls up a guy in the Volkswagen Golf, which is to a nice specification. It's the model up from the car I'm currently sat in, but it's also affordable, it's reachable. I can see myself having that car. I say to myself, "Oh wow. Yeah, I think that's the next car I'm going to have."

You look at the guy driving it and you think, "Yep, he looks like me. He's similar to me. I can do this." You don't have to have the most exotic things to want what other people have got.

Take selfies, capture moments when you're with your family and your friends. Whether you're at an event, a coffee shop doing a one-to-one, a group meeting, going to the cinema. Whether you're going to a restaurant, maybe you're surfing. Whether you're knitting or skiing. Document the moments and share it with others.

Focus mainly on value and lifestyle, and throw in the results every couple of weeks.

If you're going to do ten posts, aim for six of value, three of lifestyle, and then one of results.

The great thing about content is it won't necessarily build your business, but it can help raise credibility, influence, and also be a subtle follow-up. If you think that you can just post your way to success, you're wrong.

Remember what I said earlier, conversations come before commissions. Let's say you've already spoken to someone, but they said it wasn't for them. The content you produce can act as a subtle follow-up for people to think, "Ooh, maybe I should take a closer look. Or maybe I am missing something that I didn't quite hear the first time around. It looks like they're doing really, really well."

I'm from a small village of 35,000 people. Every year I tend to go to the same pub at Christmas time because usually people who have left the village, come back to see their family and friends, and they go into the same village, into the same pub. I remember a number of times being in the pub, bumping into old friends and acquaintances and they would say, "Frazer, I've been watching you on social media. What is it that you do because you just seem to travel all over the world, and how is the public speaking going?"

I'm then thinking, "So you see my posts, but I never see you like or comment on anything I share, why is that?"

Your friends are watching what you do, social media stalking is a thing. So just do what you need to, following the RVL formula in order to get the right message, in front of the right person, at the right time.

There's something called the value bridge. If you can imagine there's two pieces of land with a bunch of crocodiles, sharks, piranhas swimming into between the two plots of land, and there's a bridge. But this bridge is really, really, rickety. In fact, if you touch it, chances are it's going to fall down.

You're on one piece of the land, and you're calling your friends going, "Come on. It's safe. Jump over onto this side." Maybe one in very many will make the leap of faith. They'll maybe take a run up, they'll jump onto the other side because they trust you. You have influence over them. They'll get the first mover advantage.

Now from that point onwards, you have to build a value bridge. You build a bridge piece by piece to make it easier for people to come on over to the other side, because people don't want to risk getting eaten by sharks, crocodiles, or piranhas just to get over to your side to see what it is you have to offer. But if you make it such a no brainer for them, with the value that you provide, they will want to come on over to your side.

However, there's always going to be the people who try to tear your bridge down. There's always people who are going to want to see you fail. There's always going to be people saying, "Don't go with Frazer. Don't go with Bob. Don't go with Mary. They don't know what they're talking about. That bridge doesn't look so safe. The risk is not worth the reward". It's your job to keep building the bridge and getting people across the other side.

I genuinely believe the best way to do this is through Live video. There are three important things to remember when doing Live video.

The first thing is the time in which you do it. There's no point going Live at 4am on a Saturday. No one's going to watch it. Do it at primetime, anywhere from 7:00 p.m., 'til half 9:00 p.m. on Sunday, Monday, Tuesday, Wednesday, and Thursday. I've noticed that Fridays and Saturdays aren't really worth doing. If you're a Mum then morning and afternoons are also good. Remember, your target market is who you are, so if you are at home looking after your kids, then your target market will be too.

The second thing is the title. Don't just put, "I'm live." Don't just put fire emoji, fire emoji, fire emoji. Don't just say "Join me live!" Have something that's going to create curiosity. Things like, "How to...", "My three secrets to...", "My top tips to..." Maybe even, "Don't do this if you want to succeed." Or, "Don't watch this if you are happy with your life right now."

The third most important thing is the delivery.

Now I am a big fan of take away food. Chances are if it's a weekend and I don't really feel like cooking, I'll order an Indian takeaway. I know once I've eaten the food, I feel really bad. I usually have that thought, "Ugh, why did I eat that? I really shouldn't have eaten that. Why? Why? Why?"

But the real reason why I get it, is because it gets delivered to the house. I'm paying for the delivery. I'm not paying for the quality of food, because I can make better food at home. But I'm paying for the delivery, and people want the same.

More often than not people will watch and get hooked because of the delivery and the content is secondary.

Think of it this way, most people don't know the words to many songs, but they know how the beat goes. It's not what is said, but how it makes them feel. Good delivery can lead to someone feeling inspired, pumped or excited.

Now most people will face two main problems:

1. Worried about what others will think about them
2. Having no idea what to talk about

I have faced both of the above, and you or your team will face the same, so let's address them.

Worrying about what others will think about me was tough. I knew that the moment I went live my friends would have material to laugh and joke about at all future parties, gatherings and events. I remember the day I finally decided to do my first ever live video, it took me 4 months to get to the stage where I would hit the 'Go Live' button.

3, 2, 1, your live...

Within seconds I had a WhatsApp notification pop up across the top of my screen. It was my friends group chat, and the notifications were things like,

"Breaking News, Frazer is live"

"Haha this is hilarious"

"Bob has sent a photo"

"Hahahaha!"

It was so bad that I stopped the live, and deleted it.

I then reminded myself of something I had learned when I was about eighteen.

The more you think, the more you doubt, the more you doubt, the less you do, the less you do, the more you think, and so on.

I just had to get on with it. It took me another four months to do my next live.

The same thing happened, this time it was even worse, it got to me, so I stopped the live and deleted it.

I told my Dad about the situation I was dealing with, and the response was "screw it, just do it". That didn't help me. So I made the decision that I wanted to do something that would get a massive amount of attention so that I could train myself not to care about what others were thinking.

One day in 2016 I was packing my things to travel from Germany to the UK, and I had spotted my girlfriends back pack. It was a super feminine bag, slightly smaller in size, light blue in colour with many colourfully painted flowers all over them.

I asked her, "Svetlana, can I take your bag to the UK?"

Although confused, she was totally cool with it.

So I ended up packing my things in the back pack. But surely I couldn't get away with taking this bag with me. So I went to the bathroom, looked in the mirror, pointed to myself and said "Go on Frazer, I dare you!"

For the next one hundred flights I took this bag to the airport, and walked through the terminal with the bag on double straps with a crazy walk. Imagine semi lunges.

The amount of attention and crazy looks I was getting was staggering, I had trained myself not to care what other people think about me.

In fact, if you judge other people, expect other people to judge you.

I stopped judging others.

Soon after that, I made the decision to go live every single Tuesday at 9pm UK time. You can tune into the lives over on my Facebook profile.

I didn't care what my friends would say. I didn't care what the haters were posting. I didn't care if no one showed up. I just kept to it, I started to enjoy it.

Although my first live was deleted, I had eight people on it. Nowadays it's a bad live if three hundred people are watching live.

Start today, learn to not care what other people think about you. I dare you to do the crazy walk!

But what if you are ok with dealing with other people's opinions, you just don't know what to talk about?

Be sure to only talk about things you enjoy talking about, and that match up with your target market. Remember, people want to hear your side of the story, your angle, your perspective. There isn't a lot of new content these days, but everyone has a different perspective or insight. Share it.

Start by sharing your story, no one knows it more than you do.

Then you can do product demos, without sharing the product name, ask for people to contact you for more details.

I shared some title ideas above, but if you are really stuck search Google or a website called AnswerThePublic.com for different ideas.

Also if you see someone in your downline, crossline, upline or just a social media friend do a live that you like, make a note of it, and do your version of it a few weeks or months later. Be sure to give credit if you are blatantly copying it.

Just be sure to know that the most important thing about live video really is the delivery.

If you have ever seen Tony Robbins live you'll notice he claps those giant hands of his so big that I am sure atoms are created with each clap. That helps him stay in peak state. It is important for you to change your state before you hit that 'Go Live' button.

It took a few months for me to realize what changed my state. It involved me clapping as loud as I could, as fast as I could, ten times. I do it before I have to speak at an event, or before I ever do my Live videos.

However, one time, I had a problem. I was in Terminal 1 at Manchester Airport. My flight was at 10:15 p.m. but I had to go Live because it was 9pm. I thought, "How am I going to do it in the airport. I just don't think I can do my ten claps, people might think I am a terrorist".

So, I went into the toilets, walked into one of the cubicles, I closed the door, and I clapped as loud and as fast as I could ten times.

As I walked out of the cubicle to go and wash my hands, I was sharing the sink with a complete stranger who was looking at me with the most bizarre face I've ever seen. I left the toilets, went to the gate next to where my flight was departing, and I just went Live.

"Hey, hey, hey, everyone. Frazer Brookes here coming to you live from Manchester Airport and today we're going to talk to you about how to create momentum."

That live is still on my Facebook™ profile today.

I absolutely smashed it. Simply because I changed my state.

Remember to go Live each week at the same time, every single week. Be consistent with it. Remember what I said earlier, don't expect to have a shower on a Monday and be clean for the rest of the week. Have a curiosity capturing title, and then deliver it to the best you can with high energy.

On the topic of getting the right time for your content, there's no right or wrong answer. There are a lot of statistics out there that say, "Oh, the best time to post on this platform is 9:00 a.m. on a Monday, and 8:00 p.m. on a Thursday. On this platform it's 12:00 p.m. on a Friday, that's the best time post." Well, it's wrong.

The reason why is because that includes all the data from all over the world. What happens if you are from Australia and you're living in the UK, and all your audience and all your friends are in Australia? Is it a good time to post it at 7pm when it's 5am in Australia?

Probably not.

What you want to do is using the messenger feature, see how many people are online at each time, on each day. The higher the number of people who are online, the higher your overall audience will be at that time. I call this your social media rush hour.

Yes, it's not 100% accurate, but you will find that whenever the number is highest on that active list, the best initial response from my posts is greater. Using the early engagement score, if you get a lot of engagement early on in your posts, you'll get a longer engagement because you'll get a wider reach of people because the social media platform will go, "Ooh, people are liking this content. We should share it to more people." Because they're going to show posts with bigger engagement than less engagement. So be sure to reply to any comments you get on any post you do within those first ten minutes.

The final thing I will mention when it comes to creating content is aim to produce one or two pieces of content a day. I encourage you to do one in the morning, anywhere between 7am and 9am, in your time zone, and then again 7pm 'til 9pm in the evening. Just be sure it matches your social media rush hour.

If you want to improve the level of your content then I cover this a lot more in one of the resources mentioned at the end of this book.

Now it's time to go into Step 2. This is where things start to get exciting, because this is how you're going to encourage more people to come over to your profile, wanting to add you, follow you, and be your friend.

CHAPTER 7
I DARE YOU TO COMMENT DAILY (STEP 2)

You've built your foundation. You know how to create the content. Now, you have to be able to drive the traffic to the content, because if people aren't coming over to your profile and seeing what you're posting, then there's no point.

Your content will get people to think, "Oh, this person knows his stuff. Oh, this person can help me. Oh, I like this person's lifestyle," but unless people are seeing it, then they're not going to think that, so you have to be able to show people, so you have to be able to get people onto your profile, people who you didn't not know before.

Now it's time for me to introduce you to the "Toilet Technique".

This special technique is going to involve you, a phone, and a toilet. Surprise, surprise.

Three to five minutes, once, twice, three times a day, depending on how many times you visit the toilet, I want you to sit on the toilet, and I want you to get your phone out, and I want you to go into the news feed, into groups, into pages, onto the stories, onto Lives, onto the comments of your posts, and I want you to do three different types of comments.

Number one is encouragement. Number two is value, and number three is opinions.

When you're on the toilet, using the toilet time for the toilet technique, I want you to go into posts that you see and give encouragement. I want you to just go and give three fire emojis, or whatever your favourite emojis are.

Perhaps comment, "I love this" then the love heart eye emoji.

Maybe, "You rock," then the dance emoji.

Or even, "You're going to crush this" rocket emoji, rocket emoji, rocket emoji.

Go and encourage people through positivity.

The second type of post is value. If someone says that they're reading a book, The Compound Effect by Darren Hardy, go and give some value based on that conversation.

Go and say to people, "I loved the book too. I loved it when he talked about X, Y, Z. Have you ever read The Four Year Career by Richard Bliss Brooke? If you like The Compound Effect, you will love The Four Year Career."

Now, not only have you given value, but you have now contributed to the conversation, now other people might see that post and go, "Oh. I really like that idea, but who is this guy? Who is this girl?"

They click on your name. They click on your thumbnail, and they're now over onto your personal profile. They can now see your content, your results-based posts, your value-based posts, your lifestyle-based posts, your Facebook Lives, and so on.

The third type of posts are opinions. It's very important to only ever give your positive opinion. Facebook doesn't like negativity. I know negative news sells, but negativity is not going to attract the right people to you. Let's say someone says they don't know whether to wear the white dress or the black dress. Go and give your opinion.

Let's say someone says they don't know whether to go to Barcelona or go to Rome. Go and give your opinion.

Let's say someone says they don't know whether to read The Four Year Career or Beach Money by Jordan Adler. Go and give your opinion, and give reason behind your opinions, because, again, more and more people will start to see your comments.

If they agree with your opinion, they will most likely go and click on your thumbnail, click on your name, go over to your profile, check some of your comments out, your content, check your bio, check your photos, and hey, they might want to follow you, add you as a friend, or communicate in your posts.

Now, the toilet technique is the most duplicatable system on the planet, because I know for a fact that everybody reading this book right now at some point today will have already gone to the toilet or will be visiting the toilet later on, and sometimes it comes when you least expect it.

When that feeling of wanting to go to the toilet comes, you don't just say to yourself, "You know what? I'll just go tomorrow. I'll wait until Monday."

No. You do it, and the same applies with the toilet technique. You need to make the time for it. It's like brushing your teeth. It's like going to the shower. You have to do it each and every single day. It becomes a part of your routine in your business.

You're not going to take all of your business time doing this, only in small pockets of time each day. If you consistently do this you will notice your law of visibility will increase.

I dare you to start using the toilet technique, just please, don't do a live when you are there.

The same applies in groups. The more active you are in groups, the more you become a part of the community, the more the admins start to fall in love with you.

I run a group myself called The Ninja Networker VIP, which is made up of network marketers from all over the world, in over one hundred different countries, wanting to learn how to build their business using social media. Inside of our group, we have people who heavily engage in the content. They give value. They make posts, but they comment on a lot of the posts and the Lives that we do. We make note of those people, and we really appreciate those people who engage in what we're doing.

It's like us having a party, and there's one hundred people at the party, and those who are encouraging people onto the dance floor, creating good energy and good vibes through their dancing, we appreciate them, because they're adding to the atmosphere.

Let's say you're part of a dog walking group, and you're adding value. You're encouraging other dog owners or dog walkers, you're giving value to dog walkers, and you're giving your opinion to other dog walkers. The admin of that group is going to value you as a member of the dog walking group, so what can you do?

In a few weeks, in a few months, after you've been a part of that group, you're going to reach out to the group admin and say, "Hey, Mr. Admin. Hey, Mrs. Admin. I just wanted to drop by and say, thank you so much for creating this incredible group, the dog walker group. I've met so many friends, and I've had some great tips on how to walk my dog," or, "I've learnt some great places to go and walk my dog," or, "I've heard some great things to do whilst walking my dog. I just wanted to say thank you, because without you, that wouldn't become possible. How's things with you?"

What you've done there is, you've told that person, "Thank you so much." You've complimented them, and then you've looked to connect with them. In time, you can eventually develop that friendship and eventually potentially get that group admin as a customer or a distributor on your team. Think about this, just from commenting, you have been able to create new friend-ships, new eyeballs on your profile, and more traffic. This will help you increase the number of people who are in your inbox. This will help increase the number of people who watch your Lives, and this will increase the number of likes, loves, and comments, as well as shares that you get on your own posts. If you have your own group, then this will also get more people to comment in your group too.

Imagine if one group admin decides to become a distributor or a customer. You can now leverage their influence in the group to be able to build their own business, because if you go and try and add everyone in the group, first of all, it's going to take you a long time. Second of all, you'll fall into the spamming trap, where you think that it's all a numbers game.

"I'm just going to send the scripted message out to everyone in the group."

It won't work, but more important of all, won't duplicate, because it's not what you do. It's what you duplicate.

However, let's say the group admin has influence over people in the group. Let's say it's 500 people in the group. They make a post to say, "Hey, guys. I've found a fantastic product for us all to be able to use. It's going to help us with our dog walking." Let's say it's a health and wellness product. Then it's going to help, many of the group members.

The person of influence is going to recommend the product, so the people in the group, they are most likely going to listen to someone who has created the group. Founders usually have a lot of credibility.

If you encourage those people of influence to personally reach out to those they have influence over they can explode things in their business!

Remember that consistency is the key with this. You won't notice a difference after day one, day two, day three, day five. But if you continue to comment you will become an "active" user of the social media platform and you will increase your visibility, likeability, influence-ability and eventually profitability.

CHAPTER 8
I DARE YOU TO CONNECT WITH THE WORLD (STEP 3)

Network marketing is called network marketing. It's not called market networking. Building your network of connections always comes first. Build a network, and then market a product. Don't market a product and then try to network. It doesn't work that way.

You've got to have a connection, then a conversation, and then you'll get a commission.

In fact, as a Network Marketing Professional you have to collect three things:

1. Collect Friends
2. Collect Decisions
3. Collect Commissions

You are looking to find new people to become your friends. Then you are looking to ask them a fundamental question that will determine whether they will be open to checking out what you have to offer, more on that later. Then you will earn commissions from those who are going to run with it.

When the intention is for a commission from the very start, you will struggle. When the intention is for a connection, you will build a network of people which you can leverage over a period of time. Too many people in network marketing think really short term. Network marketing is mainly to create residual income, but creating residual income is a long term process.

Short term vision = short term income

Long term vision = long term income

So there are a few different ways why and how you can connect with people.

The first way is people who add or follow you. If you are creating content, and actively commenting you will see a large increase in the number of people who start adding or following you.

So what do we need to do with those people?

Let's say someone decides that they want to add you as a friend. You get a friend request. What you don't want to do is just press confirm, confirm, confirm, confirm, and think to yourself, "Well, I'm nearly at five thousand friends now because that's the magical number, because that's the absolute maximum. So if I have five thousand friends, I could make a post. If 10% of those people see it, then wow, five hundred people will like my post. And then if 10% of those people decide to click the link to join, then wow, I'm going to have fifty people join my business in one day. I'm going to be the top recruiter. I can't wait. I can't wait. I can't wait."

So people are going out there and confirming every friend

request. They're adding a hundred people a day, then getting thrown in Facebook™ jail, but they're saying it doesn't matter. "I'll do the time, because when I get out of Facebook™ jail, I'll be able to do the post." No, it does not work that way.

So when someone sends a friend request to you, you've got to go and interview them, and that is simply going over to their profile, and look out for some red flags.

Red flag number one is, do they have a default Facebook photo? If they do, then get rid.

Red flag number two, do they have no cover photo? If they don't have a cover photo, if it's a default cover photo, then get rid.

Red flag number three, are their posts sexually orientated or do they have very spammy posts? Maybe they're trying to flog some second-hand sunglasses.

Red flag number four is do they only have like a hundred friends? Now, it doesn't matter if you have a hundred friends because you might not have red flag number two, three, four, or five. Red flag number four is the last step you go to when they have an awkward profile photo and they don't have a cover photo, or their content is sexually orientated or very spammy. If they then have a low number of friends, it means that their profile is very new.

And red flag number five is go and see how many pieces of content they've actually created. If it's a low number, then it means that they just started out with Facebook™ or they've just created their profile, and that most likely means that their previous ones have been shut down.

So now let's say you come across a legitimate person. Let's say the person you accept, they've got a normal profile photo, a good cover photo, their bio looks good, their content is normal, they've got selfies in there. They've got a hundred, two hundred, three hundred, five hundred, a thousand friends. You're all good to go. So you can confirm that friend request, but do not press confirm unless you are in the situation to do the following.

1. Confirm
2. Love their profile photo - everyone loves it when they get love on their profile photo, but what it does is something crazy to the algorithm. I have noticed whenever I've loved someone's profile photo, their information and their content starts to be visible in my news feed. So if you love someone's profile photo, maybe they're going to love yours back, but what it's going to do is it's going to give you the chance, the opportunity to engage with more of their content. The best time to engage with someone's content and new friend's and new connection's content is when you've just become friends of theirs. When you give love, you will get love. If you expect people to just love your stuff without going out there and loving other people's stuff, you're going to find it very challenging.
3. Message them - send this message privately into the messenger. Don't write it on their wall. "Hey Bob, It's great to be connected with you here on Facebook™. How's things with you?" That's it. Obviously changing the name Bob to whatever it might be.

Now, I don't know about you, but if I'm in a pub and I'm drinking a beer, maybe I've just finished an event, I'm sat at the bar, and I'm having my beer. In walks a complete stranger.

Do they do option one or two?

Option one, "Hey, mate/friend. I see you're drinking alone. Could I join you?"

Or option two, "Hey, mate/friend. I see that you're drinking there on your own. Could I join you? But before I do join you, I've got an exciting opportunity to recommend you." They then open the lid of their laptop, "This company was founded in 1987 by Dr. Stevenson. With the acai berry, he created a powder which helped people with arthritis and helps them sleep better. Do you want to join this opportunity where you can earn income 73 different ways by just doing the same thing once?"

Chances are, if someone wants to be my friend, they do not pitch me. No one likes a sales pitch, but they love to hear stories, but usually to hear a story, you want to get to know the person first. That's why movies that we want to watch, whether its at the cinema or on Netflix™, we want to watch the movies with the best actors in, and the best actors to us are the people who we have seen in other movies before, the high level, A-list celebrities.

More people will watch an A-list celebrity movie than just a B-roll movie, and that's because we are hearing the story from someone we've got to know before. So the art of connection comes by just wanting to be someone's friend, not pitching them.

The second type of people to connect with are people who have liked, loved, commented, shared on one of your posts. So maybe what's happened is you've commented on a friend's post, one of their friends has seen your comment, gone over to your profile, seen a Facebook™ live you did, and has shared it, commented on it, or engaged on it. What we need to do is we need to reach out to those people. We can say something like this. "Hey, Bob. Thanks for liking, loving, commenting, sharing on my recent post. How's things with you?"

If they've loved something, they will usually be open to replying to you, especially when it's video. If someone likes or loves, comments, shares your video and you were to message them, chances are they're going to know who you are and what it's about. You're not going to have that awkwardness of, why have you added me? Why are you reaching out to me?

So I would start with anyone who shared your posts. They're going to be the warmest. The second warmest are people who comment on your posts. The third warmest are people who have engaged with your posts.

Let's use my acronym "PRICE".

P is for POST

R is for REPLY

I is for INBOX

C is for CREATE CONVERSATION AND CURIOSITY

E is for ENSURE THEY GET THE INFORMATION

So when you make a post or you comment on someone else's post the second step is to reply to any comments you see, third step is to then send them a message to their inbox. The message could be something mentioned above. Then we need to create conversation and ensure they get the information. I will cover that in the next chapters.

The third way of connecting are people who you actually find. Yes you can create content and you can comment out there, but what happens if you're in a group and you see other people's comments, you see other people's content, and you want to be their friend? Well, what you want to do is you want to first make sure you're not just going to spam and add a ton of people. If any message comes up and there's a message to say that, hey, you're adding people too fast, or do you really know this person, you want to make sure you stop adding people that day. Your goal should be adding anywhere from 8 to 10 people a day. Any more than that, you might not be able to cope or you might flag up in the social media system.

Remember, don't be a Spamela Anderson!

When you find someone, go ahead and, if you can, love and comment on any of their statuses or photos you might see. If you can't because of their settings, then don't worry. Add them, and then look to connect with them.

I have actually created a very special tool for you to find your perfect prospect based on location, sex, language and interest. More on that can be found in the resource section at the end of this book.

So let's say you find someone, whether they're in a group or whether you use my game changing tool. You love, then you comment if you can, you add them. Then you can send them a message, and you want to send them a message telling them why you're reaching out to them, why you're messaging them.

There's no point adding people and not messaging them. Most people want to know why you are adding them!

You can send a message like this:

"Hey, Bob, just reaching out to you, as I saw a post of yours pop up on my newsfeed and I loved it, so I thought it would be cool to connect. How's things?"

Or you could say,

"Hey Mary, I was just looking for people in Liverpool here on Facebook, and your profile popped up. I am currently based in Liverpool and looking to connect with more people in the area. How is things?"

Or You could say,

"Hey Sarah, I was just looking for people here on Facebook who share my passion for health and your profile popped up. I would love to connect with you. How's things?"

Or you could say,

"Hey Jim, I absolutely loved that post you made in the 'Dog Walking Group', I would love to connect with you. How's things?"

Or maybe even,

"Hey Jane, I saw a comment you made on Bob Jones' post about making cookies, loved that. Would love to connect with you. How's things?"

Do you notice a theme here? It's all about just connecting, because after you've connected with someone, you can communicate with someone. When you try to communicate with someone without connecting first, it's always awkward.

Now in the UK we get phone calls from random phone numbers, and in almost every case they are trying to sell you different products, protection, insurance etc. The conversation never goes well because you know they're just after one thing and one thing only, and that's to help them make a commission. Without connecting first, conversation is very, very difficult, and remember it's connection, conversation, commissions. We have to turn strangers into friends before we can change a friend into a business partner to become a family member.

So from now on I dare you to go out there and connect with others simply to grow a solid network of friendships.

CHAPTER 9

I DARE YOU TO COMMUNICATE WITH STRANGERS (STEP 4)

This is the part that I absolutely hated.

Being a massive introvert made it very difficult for me to enjoy speaking to people. Every time I spoke to someone, I felt uncomfortable. I felt drained. I noticed my energy levels dropping through the floor. And I just didn't like doing it.

But, the more I started to do this, the more I went through the process I'm about to share, the more I enjoyed it. And now, communicating with people all over the world is one of my favourite things to do.

In fact, one of my life mottoes now is to treat everyone like a someone.

And to do that, you have to speak to lots of different people every day. I'm going to share with you some tips and tricks to make people feel special, and to leave an imprint and a great impression on those people.

Okay. Many people, come to me and say, "Frazer, how can I be so good at communicating with people?" A lot of people who come to me, they're older than me.

At the time I'm writing this book, I'm thirty years old, and people are coming to me who are forty, fifty, sixty.

Some are married, some have been married for thirty years. Some have high-level jobs. Some people are huge leaders, but they want to get better at communicating. And it makes me laugh because every single one of them can communicate with other people, whether you have a kid, a pet, an imaginary friend, a husband, a wife, a family member, whatever it might be. You can communicate on some level.

But the goal, on social media, for network marketing, is:

To turn strangers into friends, friends into family.

So how do we do that?

I read a book that helped with relationship building and in the book the author described an acronym called FORM. It stood for Family, Occupation, Recreation, Message. I actually used the acronym for the first three or four months in my business.

The aim was to get to know someone's family, their occupation, their recreation, and their message.

But as I started to grow into the process, I realized how difficult it was for me to talk about someone else's family, when I don't have a family of my own, in terms of kids.

For example, this was how a lot of the conversations went, and it was a bit weird.

"Hey Bob, great to connect with you here on Facebook. How's things?"

"Amazing, Frazer, great to connect with you. How are you?"

"Doing amazing, thank you very much, Bob. Hey, I saw a photo. You have an awesome family. What are your kids' names?"

"Oh, one's called Mary and one's called Joseph."

"Awesome, and how old's Mary and Joseph?"

"Mary is now seven, and Joseph is five. What about you? Do you have kids?"

And I would say, "I don't have any kids. But please, tell me more about yours."

It was just a bit weird and creepy.

So I made a slight adjustment to the acronym and called it LORD.

LORD stands for Location, Occupation, Recreation, and Dreams. So it's your goal to find out a bit about where they are based, what they do for a living, what they do in their spare time, and what their goals, dreams, and aspirations are. So, it could go something like this.

"Hey Bob, great to be connected with you here on Facebook. How's things?"

"Really great, Frazer, how about you?"

"Doing fantastic, thanks, Bob. Hey, I noticed that you're over in Sydney. How's the weather over there today?"

"Oh, it's great, thanks mate. How about you? I see you're over in Liverpool."

"Yeah, the weather's not so good here; it never usually is."

"So Bob, what is it that you do for a living over in Sydney?"

"Oh, I actually am a construction worker."

"Cool. And how long have you been doing that for?"

"I've been doing that for about twenty five years now."

"Twenty five years? You must love it if you've been doing it for twenty five years."

"No Frazer, not really. I hate my boss. But it pays the bills."

If you ever hear anyone say, "But it pays the bills," bingo. You're in there. Because they are not happy with what they're doing. They're just doing it to pay the bills and you can give them an opportunity for them to get out of that rat race.

"So, Bob, what is it you do in your spare time?"

"Oh, I love playing golf. What about you, Frazer?"

"Oh, me too. I love to play golf, too. Do you get to play golf much?"

"Not as much as I'd like."

Bingo! You're in there again, because you've found something that he loves to do, but doesn't get to do it as much as he would like.

Then the last question will be like, "So Bob, have you got any plans for the rest of the year? So Bob, what's your ultimate goal? So Bob, what's your vision for the future? So Bob, what dreams do you have for you and your family?"

Now, most network marketers are used to talking about their dreams, their goals, their aspirations, their plans. But the average person isn't. And if you find someone who's not in network marketing, who likes to talk about their dreams, they know what they want, then again, bingo! You've found someone who most likely will be a great fit for your opportunity. But, if they say, "Oh, I don't really know," then you can help them with that.

If I now know where someone lives, what they do for a living, what they do in their spare time, and what their dreams, goals, and aspirations and plans are, then I am no longer a stranger to them. They are no longer a stranger to me. And now we are friends. With friends, you can then ask them what I call a 'transition question', in order to turn a friendship into a business or customer relationship.

But before we go into that, I want to give you my number one appointment generator. And in order to do this, I need you to get your phone out, and I need you to install an app on Android or iPhone called Dubsmash.

When you download this app, you're going to be able to find different songs that are 10 seconds long, where you can mime over the top.

Now here is the magic…

I want you to go and find the Happy Birthday song. It could be Marilyn Monroe Happy Birthday, it could be Stevie Wonder Happy Birthday, it could be 50 Cent Happy Birthday. What I want you to do is record the video with you miming on top. Get your kids and pets involved if you want. Record it once. Smash it out of the park just once.

Now, what you're going to do with this video, is every time it's someone's birthday, I want you write their names in a list. For example we've got Bob, Mary, Sara, Joe, and Pete.

Here is the mistake most people make. They go to those people and write a Happy Birthday message to them on their walls, in public. Something like,

"Happy Birthday, mate."

"Happy birthday. Hope you have a great day."

Some people take things to the next level and send a private message via audio message. Yeah, that's cool. But how about this…

Every single year when my birthday comes around, I get thousands of messages. It gets a little bit tiring, especially when my phone pings every few minutes.

So what I suggest you do, is contact the people on the list you have written the next day. So the day after their birthday. Send them the following message:

"Hey Bob/Pete/Mary/Joe/Sara. I can't believe I missed your

birthday yesterday. So I wanted to make it up to you..."

Then you insert the video that you recorded, using Dubsmash. Then after that, you say,

"Hope you had an awesome day. It would be great to catch up with you soon."

90% or more people who you send that video to, and that message with, will reply to you saying something like this:

"Oh my days, that was the best message I received this year. Thank you so much. It would be awesome to catch up with you soon."

You just stood out and made someone feel really special. That is just another way for you to communicate. And that is a way for you to turn a friendship into an appointment. An appointment into a potential customer or distributor.

Let's go back. You've LORD'd someone. You've turned a stranger into a friend. Now you've got to use a transition question to get talking about the business or product. Here is the transition question.

"Hey Bob. Just curious. Would you be open to checking out some more information on..." Then you've got to enter in something from the conversation that you've had with them or something more generic. And then, "No worries if not. Just thought I would ask." So here's some examples.

"Hey Bob. Just curious. Would you be open to checking out some more information on how to fire your boss? No worries if not. I just thought I would ask."

"Hey Bob. Just curious. Would you be open to checking out some more information on how to play more golf? No worries if not. I just thought I would ask."

"Hey Bob. Just curious. Would you be open to checking out some more information on how you can travel the world with your family more for less? No worries if not. I just thought I would ask."

"Hey Bob. Just curious. Would you be open to checking out some more information on how you can make money using social media? No worries if not. I just thought I would ask."

You're going to get one of three answers.

1. No
2. Yes
3. Maybe/depends what it is/Is it one of those pyramid things

So what you do if someone says "No"? You don't say, "Loser. This is a no-brainer. How can you pass this by?" No. You don't say that. You would just say,

"Hey, no worries at all, have you got any plans for the rest of the week?" So you keep the conversation going.

The majority of people are going to tell you, "No, it is not for me." That's just the way it is.

This is one stat I know for a fact. 100% of people in network marketing will hear the word "no" at least once in their journey. Everyone will hear it.

Imagine for a minute that you're a Girl Scout right now. You're a ten-year-old Girl Scout. And it's cookie-selling season. So your mum bakes a bunch of cookies for you. And now it's your job to go with a box of cookies, round the neighbourhood, and sell as many cookies as you can.

Knock-knock-knock. "Hey Mister, will you buy some of my cookies? They're $1.00 a cookie."

"No thanks."

"Okay, no worries." And move on to the next house.

"Hey Miss, will you buy one of my cookies?"

"Yes, I will."

"How many would you like?"

"I'll buy five."

"Okay, great." There's $5.

But here's the thing. There's more Girl Scouts out there, making more money than network marketers. Why? Because they're not afraid of hearing the word "no." Because they know eventually they are going to get a "yes."

So what happens if someone says, "Yes," or "Maybe."

The majority of people once they receive this sort of response are saying, "Okay, here's a link to more information. Enter link."

From this point onwards you are not allowed to send a link to more information without booking the follow up call or message.

If you've ever read Go Pro by Eric Worre, you'll know there are seven skills to becoming a Network Marketing Pro.

Finding Prospects
Inviting
Presenting
Following Up
Closing
Getting Started
Promoting Events

In this process, you will have found the prospect, invited them, presented to them, followed them up, and closed them all within maybe one day or one week. Sometimes it's less time, sometimes is more.

So someone says "Yes, I'm open, what is it?" you want to say this.

"Hey Bob, it's a visual thing. I would need to show you."

And here comes the killer part...

"Bob, when do you have fifteen minutes to take out of your life, to potentially take the rest of your life off?"

Now, that fifteen minutes is the length of a video that you can share with someone. It could be a leader video, a company overview, a product video. It could be something that gives an overview to more information, to give them a taste of what it is that you're involved with.

If it's seven minutes, say seven minutes. If it's fifteen minutes, say fifteen minutes. If it's thirty one minutes and twenty seven seconds, say thirty one minutes and twenty seven seconds.

So, "Hey Bob, it's a visual thing. When you do have thirty one minutes and twenty seven seconds to take out of your life to potentially take the rest of your life off?"

Now, I know it has the potential to take the rest of your life off. Because when I watched a fifteen minute video back in 2010, it changed my life. If I'd said "No," I would not have been in this position right now.

So, let's say they say, "Oh, I have thirty one minutes and twenty seven seconds tomorrow at 9 a.m."

"Okay, great."

So they go, "Well, what is it, what is it, what is it?"

Again, here's what I want you to understand.

Your prospect's goal is to get their questions answered before the presentation. Your goal is not to answer any of their questions until after the presentation.

"Okay I'll explain all at 9am. I will send you a message one minute to nine, with the link to the video. You're going to be finished about 9:31am. I will message you at 9:35. Does that sound fair?"

Four of the best words you can ever say in a sentence in network marketing:

"Does that sound fair?"

You will almost always get a "Yes."

So now, great. You've now found the prospect. You've turned them from a stranger into a friend. You've invited them to watch a presentation. You've booked the follow up date. And now you can close on the follow up call.

You've probably heard this saying before. "The fortune is in the follow up". But the majority of people are not creating enough scarcity and urgency for people to watch the presentation. So guess what? They follow up and they hear this message:

"I've not watched it yet. I've not seen it yet. I'll let you know when I have the time to watch it."

And then what? They don't watch it. Because there's no scarcity and urgency.

If you use what I have just shared with you, you will have created enough scarcity and urgency for people to watch the video. That doesn't mean everybody's going to message you back at 9:35am, to say, "Oh, yeah, it was great." But, you've now got a better chance.

It's so important to follow up as soon as they have seen a presentation. Here's why.

Think back to the last time you went to the cinema with your partner or friend. At the end of the movie you get out of your seats and leave the theatre. Whilst walking out of the cinema you say, "that was amazing wasn't it?"

You start to talk about the movie right after it's finished, it's fresh on the brain.

You don't say to your partner or friend after two weeks, "oh I forgot to say, how awesome was that movie we watched two weeks ago". By then you've forgotten most of it.

Get good at following up right after the presentation ends. That's one reason why in person presentations do well, whether at a home or hotel, the presentation is followed by the follow up almost immediately.

It's also important for you to make a note of everyone who says, "No", "Yes," or some form of "Maybe". Put them into a list so that you can engage with those people three or four days before you follow up with them the second, third, fourth or more time.

For example, you might have in your diary to follow up with Bob because he said "no" 8 weeks ago.

You could just call or message him on that date. Or you could go and engage on his social media posts. So your name pops up. Your face pops up. They might think, "Oh, I wonder what he's been up to. I wonder how that business thing has been going over the last few weeks."

So he goes over to your profile. He sees that you're still doing what you told him you were doing. He sees that you're living a better life. He sees that you're giving more value. He sees that you've got more likes and engagement on your posts. He sees that you are progressing.

Remember this:

Longevity creates credibility. The longer someone sees you doing the same thing for, the more credibility and trust you will create.

Now, when you follow up with them, guess what? You've got a better chance of them saying, "You know what, I'll check it out. Why not?"

I want you to understand this...

Prospecting without trust is like a car without fuel. You can stay in it all you want, but it won't get anywhere.

Trust is everything in this game. Truth plus time equals trust. Just because they said "no" today, it doesn't mean they'll say "no" tomorrow. You will hear the word "no" more than you will hear the word "yes."

I dare you to go out there and communicate with the world. I dare you to become a communication beast. I dare you to go and love on other people more than ever before.

Now you've covered how to communicate, you need to know how to close the sale, in order to grow your business, grow your commission check, and grow your freedom account.

CHAPTER 10
I DARE YOU TO CLOSE MORE (STEP 5)

I used to be terrified of closing.

I remember meeting up with friends when I first began in the network marketing industry. My dad told me to write my list of two hundred people, I managed to write one hundred and thirty seven names, and I invited four of my closest friends round to the house the day I joined.

I was excited to tell them what I had got involved in, but also I was petrified in case they thought it was a rubbish idea. I wanted to do it with my best mates.

My four friends came to the house that night and I gave probably the world's worst presentation at the time.

I feel like I blacked out as I don't remember much of it, but I was high energy, high enthusiasm, super excited and my friends were loving it. But what should have lasted twenty minutes, went on a lot longer.

I remember just going on and on and on because in the back of my head I was just thinking, "I don't know when I'm going to ask the important question of whether they want to join or not because I am so scared if they say, 'I don't want to do this.'"

I was afraid that the people I loved the most wouldn't be interested. Maybe they would start to avoid me, or even stop inviting me to things. I was overthinking it all.

When building offline, with your original list, you will be contacting and closing friends, family, acquaintances, and other people you know. This is part of the process, and should never be skipped. But, Network Marketing is a business that can be built with strangers, usually once you have the skills to do so, which in most cases you get from contacting your friends and family.

If you decide to use social media to build your network marketing business you will be able to turn strangers into friends, you will have to communicate with them, then ask if they're open. If they say yes, you've now got the right to close them because you have opened the door.

If they say, "No, screw you. This is a pyramid scheme, this is a scam. I hate this, I hate you. You're the world's worst person. Blah, blah, blah," in reality, what have you lost? You've lost a Facebook friend who you've most likely never met anyway.

Now back to our prospect Bob.

It's 9:35am, and now is the time for you to contact him, as agreed, to go through the information he saw in the video you sent him that lasted thirty one minutes and twenty seven.

A common question is, "Frazer, how should I contact Bob?"

Today there are many different ways, I like to call it the 'Ladder Of Communication". Here is the list of all the methods used by most people, starting with the most effective:

- Video Call
- Audio Call
- Video Message
- Audio Message
- Text Message

The goal is to climb the ladder of communication until you get to making a video call with your prospect.

The important thing to note is that as you climb the ladder, the power of the method increases, but the chance of making it happen decreases.

For example, it is much easier to have a text chat back and forth, but the power is less effective than that of a video call. However, although video calling is the most powerful way to communicate, it's not the easiest.

You have to start from the bottom and work your way up to the top. You can still get results without doing calls, but you will have to go through a lot more people in order to get the same effect.

After much trial and error over the years, I came up with something called the 'Parrot Principle'.

When you are beginning a conversation on social media you will most likely start with text messaging. You send a text, they send one back. After a while, you send an audio message, they reply with one back. Then you decide to send them a video message to say "hey just wanted to put a face to my voice", they don't send you one back. So you stick to audio messaging.

The idea of the Parrot Principle is you try different ways of communicating in order to climb the ladder of communication. If they follow you, you keep climbing, if they don't follow you go back down to their level and you communicate how they like.

Back to Bob.

At 9:35am you contact Bob however you agreed. Maybe it was to call him, or maybe just audio message.

What do you say?

Most people will say, "So, Bob, what did you think?"

This is the wrong thing to ask. When people are making a decision they will either think about it, or have a feeling towards it. In fact, think of it this way:

Your thoughts are your enemies, your feelings are you friends.

There's a cycle that most get trapped by. The more you think, the more you doubt. The more you doubt, the less you do. The less you do, the more you think, and so on.

So, thinking leads to doubting, doubting leads to less activity, action and decision making. Someone who is confused, someone who is trapped in their thoughts, will end up not making a decision as fast as someone who has got a feeling about something.

So, if I say to Bob, "Hey, Bob, what did you think?"

He'll probably end up saying something like,

"I think I have to think about it," or, "I think I have to think about asking my girlfriend what she thinks, so we can think together, and I'll let you know what I think."

Instead, change a couple of words and say this,

"So Bob, what did you like best?" Or "Bob, how did that make you feel?"

Then from that point onwards, you only talk about things that they bring up.

"So, Bob, what did you like best?"

"Oh, I really like the sound of the seven ways to earn", so what do you talk about? The seven ways to earn.

Once you have covered the questions he has then that panic attack feeling might come in. The close. What the heck do you say?

I struggled with this for a while, then I realised that I was only looking for people who were looking, and if they were this far in the process chances are they are fairly interested.

So after we finished with their question I would say,

"Bob, is there anything else you need to know right now in order for you to get started today?"

He might say, "Yeah. Do me a favour, tell me a little bit more about the product." Guess what you do, you tell them more about the product, then after that you would say,

"Bob, is there anything else you need to know right now in order for you to get started today?"

Bob replies, "No, no, I think I'm good."

This is where a lot of people make a mistake.

You've sold the deal and now you buy it back again. "Oh, Bob, let me tell you really, really quickly about an amazing incentive we've got going on right now, all you need to do is build seven legs with 173,000 points of volume and get three new black diamond unicorn builders, and you're going to get one free trip, not including flights, to the Dominican Republic. For you to win the second ticket, all you've got to do is get an additional two legs with 173,000 volume with an extra black diamond unicorn builder".

You've lost them. People will get confused and guess what, when they're confused, they're in a thinking state. When they're in a thinking state, they are doubting. When they're doubting, they are not taking action.

So what do you say when someone is done with their questions?

"Great, sounds like you're ready to get started."

That's it. Keep it simple. There's no complex sales tactic to use. In golf, if you want to hit the ball further you don't hit the ball harder, you use another club. In Network Marketing if you want to get more people to join your business, you speak to more people.

As soon as they say they are ready to join then get the laptop open, or guide them to the enrolment page. Walk them through it. Don't go, "Okay, well let me book you in for next week." No. If someone says yes now, they're ready to buy now.

Let's think of it this way, I'm in a supermarket and I've got my vegetables, I've got my pasta, I've got my chicken in the basket. I'm walking to the counter and I think, "Oh, I'd really fancy some popcorn," and I put it in my bag and I go to the cashier and I go, "Oh, actually, can we book me in for next week and I'll come back and get the popcorn?" No. You buy it there, you want it, you're ready for it, you get it, you buy it. If you don't, chances are that you won't buy the popcorn at the arranged time.

If you really want to dramatically increase your chances of getting a yes from your prospects so that they become a distributor or customer then you need to use three way messaging. If you think you are too big for help in this industry, you will lose long-term.

There is a very tiny percentage of people who have had massive success without help or guidance. The help usually comes from your upline, side line or maybe, if a company's new, maybe even one of the corporate members of the company.

You want to do this with what's called a three-way messenger chat. If you are on a voice call or a video call, then you want to invite your upline, your supporter, your contributor, your fellow impactor, into the conversation. If it's a text, audio, or video chat, not a call, you want to go in and add your upline into the conversation.

Now, there is you, your prospect/friend, and your upline supporter/impactor/friend. Okay, so there's three people in the group, hence, three-way call/chat. And that can grow to four-way call, five-way call, whatever, the more and more people get involved in the conversation.

It's your job to introduce your friend to your upline by edifying your upline so they look as good as possible to create the element of trust between the stranger and your upline.

It could go something like this:

"Hey, Bob, I just wanted to introduce you to my mentor, my friend, my supporter, my collaborator, Dave. Dave is a fantastic individual, he's helped me every single step of the way, but he's also been able to do X, Y, and Z. If you have any other questions, feel free to ask him too."

Message one done.

Second message.

"Hey, Dave, I just wanted to introduce you to my awesome friend Bob. Me and Bob, got to know each other on Facebook three months ago, two days ago, a week ago, earlier today (whatever it might be). He's totally open to the idea, he's seen the presentation, and he has some questions. Can you share your vision, your belief, and your mission with what we're doing? I'd really appreciate it. Thanks so much."

What you've done there is you've told your upline that your friend is totally open to the idea, they've seen a presentation, and they're this far in the process. The contributor, supporter, upline now knows, they just have to do their part. They've just got to answer some questions and share their story just to help this person seal the deal.

Meanwhile, Bob, your friend, is looking at this situation and thinking, "I'm going to get so much support. But these guys, they seem really cool. They seem like they're doing better in life than I'm doing right now. Maybe they can help me get what I want. Maybe they can help me fire my boss. Maybe they can help me play more golf. Maybe they can help me and my family live our dreams."

That is how this works.

So in summary.

- On the follow up call ask, "What did you like best?"
- Only answer the questions that they bring up
- Introduce them to your upline in a three-way chat or a three-way call
- Ask, "Bob, is there anything else you need to know right now in order for you to get started today?"
- Then say, "Great, sounds like you're ready to get started."

If you go through the five step process I've just walked you through, and you do it every single day, the results you get have the potential to be incredible.

CHAPTER 11
I DARE YOU TO DO IT

If you focus on producing content five minutes a day, you comment three to ten minutes a day, you connect with new people, you communicate with existing people, and you're closing the people who are open. If you do that day in, day out, day in, day out, with time you will see a huge difference.

But it will take time.

You will deal with haters. Your friends might think you are crazy. Your partner might not agree with you doing what you're doing. You might even get some resistance from your upline.

But it works.

Focus on your progression, don't look for perfection. The day you become perfect is the day you will lose on social media, people want to see you for who you really are.

Authenticity is, and always will be your number one weapon.

People will copy many of your posts in time, and they won't

give you credit. But no one can copy your personality.

Social media is an incredible tool that can be a huge help for network marketers, but only if it is used correctly. If you follow what I have shared in this book, in time you will become a professional and will stand out from most.

During my research into this incredible industry I have found that if you get one decision a day, you can look, depending on compensation plans, to earn roughly around $1,000 a month in commissions.

If you get two decisions a day, you can look to earn about $2,000 a month in commissions.

If you get five decisions a day, you can look to earn anywhere from around $5,000 a month.

Guess how many decisions you need to collect to earn $25,000 a month? Twenty five decisions a day.

Now, a decision is simply yes or no. The catch is that it's going to take you some time to get paid. You don't get paid the amounts above on a yes and a no right now. You might get a fast start bonus, but the big money is not in the fast order bonus. The big money is in the duplication.

Some will, some won't, so what because there are some people out there who want what you've got.

Now the numbers when using social media will be slightly higher, you can expect to get more "no's", than "yes's" online so you will have to do more work, but that work can be done from home, on your phone.

But, do not neglect the other methods of building your business. Don't think that you can skip the live in-person events. Don't ever think you know it all.

This industry thrives off collaboration. Like-minded people wanting more from life, and for the chance to help another person better their lifestyle.

Network marketing is the most valuable industry on the planet. It really is a way for you to break free. To be completely yourself and for you to impact the world on a massive scale.

I dare you to use social media to build your business.

I dare you to put the five step process into practice.

I dare you to be 100% yourself.

I dare you to create content daily.

I dare you to use your time on the toilet wisely.

I dare you to walk through an airport doing a crazy walk with a strange backpack on.

I dare you to connect with the world.

I dare you to communicate with more strangers than you've ever done before.

I dare you to ask the transition question.

I dare you to fall in love with the person you are, and the one you are becoming.

I dare you to collaborate with others.

I dare you to live the life of your wildest dreams.

I dare you to go and impact your neighbour.

I dare you to go and be a legend.

I dare you to attend your company convention.

I dare you to give your family every single thing they want and more.

I dare you to use your time on social media wisely.

I dare you to share this book with other people in your team and your future team so they can discover the exact strategy to grow their businesses.

I dare you.

I double-dare you.

I triple-dare you.

FURTHER RESOURCES

I DARE YOU COMMUNITY:

For more content, updates, how to access the game changing tool and "dares" for you to grow your business using social media, join our dedicated Facebook group for everyone who has bought the I Dare You book.

Facebook.com/groups/Idareyoubook

TUESDAY LIVES:

Join me every Tuesday at 9pm UK time as I go live sharing different "How To" training for you to become a Network Marketing Ninja!

Facebook.com/fbrookes

SOCIAL MEDIA PLATFORMS:

Facebook Profile: Facebook.com/fbrookes
Instagram: instagram.com/frazer.brookes
YouTube: YouTube.com/channel/frazerbrookesonline
Facebook Page: Facebook.com/frazerbrookesonline

FREE ONLINE MASTERCLASS:

Discover how you can become the next Network Marketing superstar by joining Frazer on one of his upcoming online masterclasses where he walks through some fundamental tweaks you can make to your business to start seeing the results you deserve.

Go to FrazerBrookes.com/Masterclass and reserve your seat.

SUCCESS SUMMIT:

Every year Frazer holds one of the biggest generic Network Marketing events in the world. Success Summit has been designed to raise the professionalism of the industry and to bring the best strategies that are working for top performers from many different companies and countries.

For more on Success Summit go to SuccessSummit.info

WANT TO GIVE YOUR ORGANISATION COPIES OF *I DARE YOU?*

Go to frazerbrookes.com/buybooks and select your order.

For more products by Frazer go to
FrazerBrookes.com/products

MY FINAL DARE FOR YOU...

If you enjoyed reading the book, write a post on social media along with a photo of you holding the book, to let people know how much you loved it. Use #IDareYouBook as I will be checking all posts using the hashtags regularly to see any cool reviews.

WANT FRAZER TO TRAIN YOUR ORGANISATION?

Frazer can coach and train your organisation in a number of ways, but most common are:

- Live Event - whether it's a company convention, team event, leadership retreat or other.
- Online Calls - whether on Zoom or via Facebook Live into a closed group.

Frazer specialises in:

- Social Media
- Mindset
- Core Skills
- Leadership

If you would like Frazer to train your organisation send an email to info@frazerbrookes.com

NOTES